UNITED STATES
HISTORY

Volume I   *1620—1900*

BY STEPHEN LEWIN

A Pacemaker® Book

Fearon Education
Belmont, California

Simon & Schuster Supplementary Education Group

Designer: Terry McGrath

Photo credits:

All illustrations and photographs: THE BETTMANN ARCHIVE

Series editor: Joseph T. Curran

ISBN–0–8224–7681–9

Library of Congress Catalog Card Number: 85–50811

Printed in the United States of America

1. 9 8 7 6 5

Contents

Here's a good place
at the corner,
I must stand and
see the show.

WALT WHITMAN

Chapter 1

The Search for Freedom

Words to Know

colony   place where people from somewhere else settle; the people who live in a colony keep some of their ties with their old country

debtors   people who owe money

empire   different areas under the rule of a single government; these areas are beyond the borders of the ruling country

foreign   from another country

jury   a group of people who decide if a person on trial is guilty or not guilty

loyal   faithful to

natives   people who live in the place where they were born

rebels   people who fight control by the government

representatives   people who are chosen to speak or act for others

settlers   people who come to live in a new place

treaty   an agreement between two groups of people (usually a written statement)

They called it the "Time of Death." They were the Pilgrims, a small group of English people living in a land they knew almost nothing about. Their ship, the *Mayflower*, had reached the shores of Plymouth, Massachusetts, in late November of 1620. They'd come with almost nothing—"no butter or oil, not even a sole to mend a shoe." There was no time to plant crops before the winter cold set in. With the cold came sickness. Day after day, the Pilgrims watched sadly as men, women, and children died. Only half of them lived through that first winter. Yet they did not give up. They had come to this "New World" to be free to worship God in their own way, and that gave them hope.

The Pilgrims were not alone in their new land. They knew that other people—**Native** Americans, or "Indians," as they were called by Europeans—lived in the area. The Pilgrims had seen them, but they had never spoken to them.

One evening in the spring, as the Pilgrims were meeting, an amazing thing happened. One of the natives walked into their gathering and said, "Hello," in English. "I am Samoset," he told them. The Pilgrims stared at him. Samoset explained that he had learned a little English from the crews of English fishing ships. He said that his friend Squanto, who spoke even better English than he did, wanted to help the Pilgrims.

Squanto came to Plymouth the next day. He introduced the Pilgrims to Massasoit, the most powerful leader in the area. Massasoit and the Pilgrims worked out a **treaty** to keep the peace. Unlike later treaties between **settlers** and Indians, this one lasted 50 years. In the following months, Squanto taught his Pilgrim friends how to live in the New World. He taught them the best way to plant beans, corn, and pumpkins. He showed them how to trap deer and how to tap maple trees for syrup.

From the Old World to the New

Things went well for the Pilgrims now. By the next fall, they knew they had grown enough food for winter. The Pilgrims decided to celebrate their good harvest. They invited Massasoit and began preparing a meal of deer, geese, and wild turkey. When the day for the feast came, the Pilgrims were surprised to see Massasoit arrive with about 90 friends. The Pilgrims did not have enough food for everyone. Massasoit saw their concern and sent out his braves to hunt. Soon they returned with five more deer. Then the feast began. Everyone enjoyed it so much that it lasted for three days. From this we get the story of the first Thanksgiving Day.

Plymouth was not the first **foreign** settlement in the Americas. But we think of it as special because it was founded by Europeans seeking freedom. Though their early years were hard, the Pilgrims soon learned to work the land. They were able to live and worship as they pleased. In time, their settlements spread out from Plymouth.

The success of the Pilgrims led others wanting freedom to come here. Most of them gave up everything they had to make a fresh start in America. Some, like the Pilgrims, wanted freedom to practice their religion. The **colony** of Maryland, for example, was set up so that English Catholics could worship freely. Other settlers wanted to escape poverty or to make their own laws. Georgia was founded so that **debtors** could settle in America rather than go to prison in England.

The Puritans

Like the Pilgrims, the Puritans had suffered in England because of their religion. In the 1630s, they began several settlements on Massachusetts bay. The most important of these was Boston. The Puritans did well in Massachusetts, and their settlements fanned out around the bay. But they did not allow others the freedom they had found. They made all people who lived in their settlements follow strict Puritan ways.

Those who did not agree with the Puritan leaders were often badly treated. Roger Williams was a minister who held many unpopular views. He believed that the Indians should be paid for the land the settlers took. He also believed that all people should have the right to worship as they wished. Today, all Americans have freedom of religion. But that was not the case in Williams's time.

Roger Williams

The Puritan leaders finally decided they had had enough of Williams. They ordered him to leave. Williams lived with the Indians for a while. Then he decided to start his own settlement. Today it is the state of Rhode Island.

Other people who angered the Puritan leaders also were forced to leave. Anne Hutchinson was thrown out when she claimed it was more important to lead a holy life than to obey Puritan leaders. She left with her followers in the dead of winter and settled near what is now New York City.

Anne Hutchinson

Three hundred years ago, the Quakers in England had few rights. They did not belong to the Church of England, and they would not fight in England's wars. For this, they were often beaten, jailed, or even hanged.

The world of the Quakers was a far cry from the world of William Penn. He was the son of a rich man and a friend of Charles II, the king of England. He was able to enjoy everything England had to offer someone in his position. Yet there came a time when Penn was won over to the Quaker view of life. He decided to join them. Many people were not happy with his choice. One man told Penn, "You must give the Quakers up or spend your life in prison." Penn replied by saying, "Then my prison shall be my grave."

Penn did spend some time in jail for his Quaker views. But he would not give them up. In fact, he decided to make it his life's work to find a safe place for the Quakers to live.

One day, Penn went to the king with a surprising offer. Charles II owed Penn a lot of money. Penn said that instead of money, he would rather have a large piece of land in America. There he would set up a "free colony to help all mankind." The king was glad to pay Penn with something he had a lot of—land—rather than with something he had little of—money. So in 1681, the colony of Pennsylvania ("Penn's Woods") was founded.

William Penn's Free Colony

William Penn and American Indians

Pennsylvania became a special place of freedom. All the people there had freedom of religion. They had the right to a trial by a **jury** if they were charged with a crime. Penn also insisted that the Indians be treated fairly. It was the Indians who had welcomed the settlers here. They had made it possible for the newcomers to live well in America. But then the Europeans took over the homelands of the Native Americans.

Pennsylvania was to be a place where people of many different backgrounds could live together in peace. They came from such places as England, Scotland, Ireland, the Netherlands, Germany, France, and Finland. They were Protestants, Catholics, and Jews. No matter what their differences were, all people had the same rights.

A New Person— the American

In the year 1760, George III became king of England. An important part of his **empire** was in North America. There, 13 colonies lay along the Atlantic coast, from New Hampshire in the north to Georgia in the south. Though the ways of life were very different in the 13 colonies, the people were alike in many ways.

Self-Image. In the 140 years since the landing of the *Mayflower,* the people in the colonies had come to depend on themselves rather than on Europe. They had stopped thinking of themselves as English, German, or Swedish. Now they were Pennsylvanians, Georgians, or New Yorkers. Or they may even have thought of themselves simply as Americans.

Religious Freedom. The Americans had come to believe that no matter what their religion was they should be able to practice it in peace. Most Americans believed that people had a right to their different views. After all, they said, all people were equal in the eyes of God.

Self-Government. The Americans felt they had the right to govern themselves. This did not mean they wanted to be free of England. In fact, most of them were very **loyal** to England. But they believed that they should be able to elect their own **representatives** to government. These representatives would decide such things as which taxes Americans would have to pay.

Trial by Jury. In all the colonies, people accused of a crime had the right to a trial by jury. The Americans believed that this would help to make the trials fair.

King George III

A New King— and Some Important Changes

When George III became king of England, he felt that all he needed from the Americans was their loyalty. But a war was going on in both Europe and North America. As we will see in the next chapter, when that war ended, George decided to make some major changes. Because of this, many Americans turned against him. They became **rebels,** and King George was soon faced with the American struggle for independence.

EXERCISE 1

Fill in the circle beside the words that best complete each of the following statements.

1. During their first winter in America, the Pilgrims
   ⓐ harvested a big crop.
   ⓑ suffered from sickness and hunger.
   ⓒ spread out around Massachusetts Bay.

2. Things changed for the Pilgrims in the spring when
   ⓐ their crops rotted.
   ⓑ war broke out between the Indians and the Pilgrims.
   ⓒ Squanto arrived to help the settlers.

3. The Pilgrims came to America to have the freedom to
   ⓐ worship as they pleased.
   ⓑ elect their own representatives.
   ⓒ own land.

4. Roger Williams and Anne Hutchinson
   ⓐ founded settlements in Rhode Island and New York.
   ⓑ returned to England.
   ⓒ started their own religions in Massachusetts.

5. Georgia was founded so that
   ⓐ Catholics could practice their religion freely.
   ⓑ farmers could find rich soil in which to grow their crops.
   ⓒ debtors would have a place to settle rather than go to prison in England.

6. When William Penn said, "Then my prison shall be my grave," he meant he would
   ⓐ stay in prison until the king gave him his money.
   ⓑ not give up his Quaker views.
   ⓒ work to make things better for debtors.

7. Pennsylvania was a special colony because

    ⓐ only Quakers had many freedoms.

    ⓑ it became free of English control.

    ⓒ people of many different backgrounds could live together in peace.

8. In 1760, the colonists did *not* feel the need to

    ⓐ practice their religion.

    ⓑ be free of England.

    ⓒ have trials by jury.

Answer the questions below.

9. What did the Pilgrims learn from Squanto?

    _____

    _____

    _____

10. Who gave Native Americans the name "Indian"?

    _____

11. Although Plymouth was not the first foreign settlement in the Americas, we think of it as special. Why?

    _____

    _____

Thomas Jefferson, author of the Declaration of Independence
and third president of the United States

Chapter 2

The Road to Independence

Words to Know

declaration   a public statement; the Declaration of Independence gave notice of America's independence from England

delegates   people chosen to speak or act for others

independent   free from rule by others

massacre   the brutal killing of many people

Parliament   the part of the British government that makes laws

petition   a written request signed by many people asking for changes

"**K**ill the soldier! Kill the coward!"

It was a cold winter evening in 1770, and trouble was in the air. An angry group of Americans had gathered in the streets of Boston. They were yelling at a British soldier. Earlier that day, the soldier had hit a young boy with his gun. The Americans were cursing and shouting. They walked toward the soldier.

"Knock him down! Kill him! Kill him!"

The man yelled for help. Seven British soldiers came running. The mob pressed forward, shouting insults and throwing snowballs. "Cowards! Let's see you fire! You wouldn't dare!"

By now the crowd was growing. Many of the people had sticks in their hands and swung them at the soldiers. The soldiers backed up. They looked frightened. One of them was hit by a rock thrown from the mob. Suddenly the British started shooting wildly. When the smoke cleared, five men lay dead in the snow. The British were about to fire again when an officer ran in front of them and ordered them not to. The Americans pulled away into the darkness, shouting curses. Soon, all over town, church bells were ringing loudly. More people came out into the streets. "Murder! **Massacre**!" The words were on everyone's lips.

The Americans did not soon forget this "Boston Massacre."

The British Clamp Down

In the last chapter, we read how the Americans were loyal to George III when he became king of England in 1760. By 1770, many of them were cursing his name. What happened to change their minds? Why were they angry?

To understand how this happened, we must go back to 1763. In that year, the French and Indian War ended. The Americans and the British had defeated the French and some Indian tribes. The war had cost a lot of money. England decided to make the Americans help pay for it by placing new taxes on them.

In 1765, the British **Parliament** passed the Stamp Act. This meant the colonists would have to buy stamps to put on such things as newspapers and playing cards. Many Americans were angered by this. They felt the British had taken away their right to set their own taxes.

Parliament finally canceled the Stamp Act. However, in a few months it voted in new taxes. Also, it sent more soldiers to make sure the colonists paid. This caused some leading Americans to send **petitions** to King George. The letters said, "We are loyal to you. We are British subjects. Just give us back our rights. That is all we ask!"

The British soldiers in the cities caused much trouble. There were many fights, the worst of which was the Boston Massacre. As we have seen, the Americans were as much at fault as the British. However, stories of the "massacre of peaceful Americans" spread over the colonies and raised strong feelings against the British. There were people in England who were afraid that Britain could lose its American colonies if it kept passing such tough laws. But King George was not one of them. He ordered Parliament to place a special tax on tea.

The Boston Tea Party

In 1773, a ship loaded with British tea reached Boston. Late one night, a group of colonists dressed themselves as Indians and boarded the British ship. They threw all the tea into the water. The Boston Tea Party, as this was called, was almost the last straw for the British. They decided to make an example of the people of Boston. They wanted to show once and for all who was the boss. Parliament drew up new taxes for Massachusetts. Also, it closed the Boston harbor, which forced many people out of work. Finally, the British sent a large number of troops to make sure the new laws were followed.

Leaders from all the American colonies met in Philadelphia in September of 1774 to decide what to do. There the **delegates** heard Patrick Henry of Virginia say, "The differences between Virginians, Pennsylvanians, New Yorkers, and New Englanders are no more. I am not a Virginian, but an American."

When King George heard about this meeting, he knew there would be trouble. "I will make them give in," he said. But the Americans were not ready to give in. In Massachusetts, angry colonists formed groups called "Minutemen." These men, between the ages of 16 and 60, agreed to turn out at a minute's notice when there was danger. The Minutemen began storing guns and bullets in Concord, a town 20 miles outside Boston.

The angry feelings were about to explode. In April of 1775, the British general Thomas Gage decided on a surprise raid to destroy the American guns at Concord.

Late on the night of April 18, about 1,000 British soldiers quietly left Boston. They thought that no one had seen them. But they were wrong. Some Americans had spotted their movement.

I Am . . . an American!

Patrick Henry

In Lexington, the townspeople slept peacefully while a few soldiers kept guard. Suddenly, from out of the darkness, Paul Revere rode up shouting. He rode from house to house, warning that British troops were on the march. After waking the town, he met up with William Dawes. Together they rode toward Concord, giving the alarm as they went.

They were stopped by a group of British soldiers. Revere and Dawes were captured, but another man, Dr. Samuel Prescott, got away to spread the warning. Through the long night, Minutemen began reaching Lexington and Concord.

All the while, the British marched toward Lexington, thinking they would surprise the town. Day was just breaking when they arrived. Waiting at the village green were about 40 Minutemen drawn up in a line.

Captain John Parker, the American leader, gave his men last-minute orders. "Stand your ground. Don't fire unless fired upon, but if they want a war, let it begin here!"

"If They Want a War, Let It Begin Here!"

Paul Revere

North Bridge, Concord

A shot rang out from the British side, and then the whole British line began firing. Eight Americans fell dead. As the smoke from the guns rose over Lexington, the Americans broke and ran. The British, now in high spirits, pushed on toward Concord.

There, about 450 Minutemen had gathered on high ground outside of town. The British took Concord without firing a shot. They began piling up the American guns and supplies to burn them. When the Minutemen saw the flames, they thought the British were burning the town. They hurried to try to save it.

As the Americans neared the North Bridge, the British started firing. But instead of stopping, the Americans came racing across the bridge. Now it was the British turn to break and run.

It was getting late, and the British still had to get back to Boston. Their march was a time of terror. The whole country seemed to rise up against them. The Americans hid behind trees and stone walls, firing shot after shot. Toward the end, many British soldiers simply threw away their guns and ran. By the time they reached safety, about 300 British and 80 Americans had been killed or hurt.

News of the battles at Lexington and Concord surprised everyone. Farmers and storekeepers without training had stood up to the powerful British army. And they'd beaten it. The Minutemen had proved that Americans were willing to die for a cause they believed in.

Less than a month later, leaders from all the colonies gathered again in Philadelphia. They called their meeting the Second Continental Congress. The delegates did not want war with Britain. Still, American blood had been spilled. The delegates decided to ask England for peace. But at the same time, they got ready to go to war.

First they named a Virginia planter, George Washington, to lead the American army. Washington was well known as a brave soldier. He had led a group of Americans during the French and Indian War. Since there were really no American troops other than the Minutemen, Washington's first job was to build an army.

At the same time, the Congress sent King George a long petition complaining of the way the British had treated them. The king's answer was angry. He sharply attacked the Americans and got laws passed that said Britain would no longer protect the colonies. Worst of all, he sent 30,000 new troops.

Now the Americans felt they had only one choice. In June of 1776, the Congress gave an important job to Thomas Jefferson, a young delegate from Virginia. Jefferson was asked to write a **declaration** that would tell why the colonies should be **independent** from Britain.

"Why me?" Jefferson asked.

He was answered by his friend John Adams. "You can do the job ten times better than anyone else in this hall," Adams said.

"Well," said Jefferson, "if you are sure, then I will do the job as well as I can."

He did it very well indeed. Jefferson's Declaration of Independence was a ringing call to people all over the world who wanted to be free. On July 4, 1776, the Americans gave notice that, "these United Colonies are, and of right ought to be, free and independent States."

They had finally declared their independence from the British. Now all they had to do was win it.

The War Begins

EXERCISE 2

Match each statement on the left with the person on the right who might have said it.

1. _____ "You can do the job ten times better than anyone else in this hall."

2. _____ "The differences between Virginians, Pennsylvanians, New Yorkers, and New Englanders are no more. I am not a Virginian, but an American."

3. _____ "I will make them give in."

4. _____ "The British are coming!"

5. _____ "Stand your ground. Don't fire unless fired upon, but if they want a war, let it begin here!"

6. _____ "Well, If you are sure, then I will do the job as well as I can."

a. Thomas Jefferson

b. John Adams

c. Captain John Parker

d. Patrick Henry

e. King George

f. Paul Revere

Answer the questions below.

7. What touched off the Boston Massacre?

_____

_____

8. Why did England pass the Stamp Act?

_____

_____

_____

_____

9. Which right did Americans feel they lost when England passed the Stamp Act?

_____

10. How did England react to the Boston Tea Party?

_____

_____

_____

11. Who were the Minutemen?

_____

_____

_____

12. What happened to Paul Revere and William Dawes when they tried to warn the people of Concord that British soldiers were approaching?

_____

_____

_____

13. What was surprising about how the battles of Lexington and Concord turned out?

_____

_____

14. At the Second Continental Congress, who was chosen to lead the American army?

_____

15. How did King George respond to the petition that the Second Continental Congress sent him?

_____

_____

_____

_____

Chapter 3

The American Revolution

Late on Christmas Day in 1776, darkness was falling as a group of men marched silently to the Delaware River. It was terribly cold. For three hours, the men waited on the banks as small groups were rowed across from Pennsylvania to New Jersey. The river was filled with large chunks of ice. Sometimes the boats almost tipped over. Ice formed on the oars. The men had to scrape it off to be able to keep on rowing. The water was so cold that anyone falling overboard would die in a few minutes.

At three different points, Americans were silently crossing the Delaware River that night. It was well after three in the morning before they were all across. Then the army began its march through the darkness to the village of Trenton. A force of Hessians, Germans fighting for the British, was stationed there. George Washington knew the Hessians would have spent Christmas drinking and enjoying themselves.

He planned a surprise attack for just after dawn. If the Americans could get to Trenton unnoticed, they might be able to capture the Hessians. If the plan were to fail, the war could be lost. It was Washington's biggest **gamble.**

There were more than nine miles between the river and Trenton. The snow was blowing and drifting. The wind cut through the light clothing the Americans were wearing. Many of the soldiers walked with rags tied around their feet. They left bloody footprints in the snow.

As the Americans marched, the Hessians slept. After a day and night of drinking, the Hessians were in no shape to fight a battle. At eight in the morning, the Americans charged. Before the Hessians were out of their beds, the Americans had gained control of the town. They cut off all escape routes. In a few minutes, the battle was over. The Americans took more than 900 **prisoners.** More importantly, they won their first victory since declaring their independence from Britain.

A Hopeless Cause?

Until Trenton, things had not gone well for the Americans. In battle after battle, they were beaten by the more powerful British. The worst defeat was at New York. The Americans lost the city, and more than 3,000 of their soldiers were taken prisoner.

Still more defeats followed the loss of New York. Washington's army **retreated** south, with the British hot on their heels. The Americans seemed to have no fight left in them. Many people wondered if the right person had been chosen to lead the army. Was Washington really a good general? Could the British be defeated? Wouldn't it be better to give in and follow the king's rule? Many Americans lost heart.

The coming of winter saved the Americans. Often in those days, armies did not fight in bad weather. General Howe, the leader of the British army, took his force back to New York to wait for warmer weather. That's when Washington got the idea for a surprise attack on the Hessians at Trenton.

American spirits were high after that battle. Now the Americans had some hope that they could beat the British. Yet the battle didn't solve any of the real problems. Britain was still the world's most powerful country. The British were well armed and well trained. They had more than 50,000 soldiers in North America. The Americans had only about 10,000.

And the Americans were deeply divided. Many wanted to remain a part of Britain and were against the war. Some of these **Loyalists** fought in the British army.

The Americans were not trained soldiers, either. They were farmers, store owners, and craftsmen who had taken up arms to fight for a cause they believed in. Many of their leaders had never fought in a war. The **Patriots** didn't have enough guns, food, or heavy winter clothing. Washington had to beg Congress for the money to buy these things. Many Americans had joined the army for only a few months. They planned to go home when their time was up. Washington was not sure he could keep the army going.

For almost two years after the battle of Trenton, the British chased the American army from one colony to the next. Again and again, they beat the Americans in small battles. But they couldn't trap them. Each time, Washington got his troops just out of their reach.

Still, the American army kept getting smaller. The soldiers got tired of the fighting and the retreating. When they had served their time, many of them left.

Washington's troops in New York

The Low Point: Valley Forge

The worst time was during the winter of 1778. The British stayed in Philadelphia, warm and well fed. About 20 miles away, at a place called Valley Forge, the Americans lived in tents. Many did not have warm clothes or blankets. Some did not have shoes. You could tell where the army had been, Washington said, by the blood in the snow. About 2,500 Americans died from cold and sickness during that long winter. Many others lost heart and went home.

If the British had attacked the American army then, they might have won the war. But they stayed in Philadelphia. While the British waited for spring, the Americans received important help. France had decided to join the war against Britain. The French had a well-trained army and a strong navy. They also had money to help the Americans buy food and clothing.

Deborah Sampson

Deborah Sampson and George Washington

In March of 1781, 21-year-old Robert Shurtleff walked into an army post in a small Massachusetts town and signed up. With a group of other soldiers, Shurtleff traveled south and joined Washington's troops near New York. Robert Shurtleff seemed to be much like the rest of the soldiers in camp. What no one knew at the time was that "Robert Shurtleff" was really a young woman named Deborah Sampson. For years Deborah had wanted to fight for the Americans. But women weren't allowed in the army. She had **disguised** herself as a man so that she could **enlist.**

Deborah Sampson fought well. In battles along the Hudson River, she suffered a sword cut on her head and a bullet wound in her leg. To keep from being found out, she cared for the wounds herself.

The World Turned Upside Down

In the spring of 1781, the fighting switched to the south. The British general, Lord Cornwallis, marched his army through Virginia, capturing and burning towns. At Yorktown, he waited to pick up food and arms. Yorktown is on a **peninsula** in the Chesapeake Bay. Washington thought he might be able to trap Cornwallis there and end the war. He asked the French navy to sail south to close off the bay. The American and French armies moved quickly from New York to Yorktown.

Deborah Sampson marched with Washington's army. French and American soldiers cut off the British escape by land. In a bloody night battle, Deborah helped capture an important hill overlooking the British camp.

Cornwallis now saw that there was no way to escape. On October 16, 1781, Deborah Sampson and the others listened as a British drummer tapped out a call for a meeting. Suddenly, the battlefield grew silent. In a few minutes, a British officer rode up to Washington's tent with a **surrender** note. On October 19, the British put down their arms and marched out of their camp. As they left, their band played a song called "The World Turned Upside Down." For the world's most powerful country, the world had indeed turned upside down.

Shortly after the battle, Deborah Sampson came down with a high fever. She tried to take care of herself, but she was too weak. Her secret was finally discovered by a doctor. A surprised army then sent her home. After the war, Deborah married and had three children. Never again did she have to fight for her country. But she never grew tired of telling the story of her days as a soldier in George Washington's army.

Cornwallis surrendering to George Washington

Yorktown turned out to be the last battle of the American Revolution. Though King George wanted to go on fighting, he saw that the British people were tired of war. In 1783, the British and the Americans signed a peace treaty.

The Americans had fought and defeated the world's most powerful country. They had won because they felt they had a cause worth fighting for. They had gained their freedom. But now they had to form a government that would keep them free, strong, and **unified.** This would prove to be as hard as winning independence.

A Free Country

EXERCISE 3

Fill in the circle beside the word or words that best complete each of the following statements.

1. To get to Trenton, the Americans had to cross the _____ River.
   - ⓐ Delaware
   - ⓑ Hudson
   - ⓒ Chesapeake

2. At Trenton, the Americans captured a force of _____ soldiers.
   - ⓐ British
   - ⓑ French
   - ⓒ Hessian

3. When Washington heard that the British were camped at Yorktown, he asked for help from _____ .
   - ⓐ Benjamin Franklin
   - ⓑ the French navy
   - ⓒ the Hessians

4. At Yorktown, British forces under _____ surrendered to the Americans.
   - ⓐ Robert Shurtleff
   - ⓑ General Howe
   - ⓒ General Cornwallis

5. After Yorktown, _____ wanted to go on fighting.
   - ⓐ Washington
   - ⓑ King George
   - ⓒ the British people

6. In 1783, the British signed a _____ which said that the United States was independent.
   - ⓐ treaty
   - ⓑ contract
   - ⓒ pass

Answer the questions below.

7. What happened at the battle of New York?

_____

_____

_____

8. What were those Americans who supported the British called?

_____

9. What were those Americans who fought the British called?

_____

10. In 1778, the American army spent a long, hard winter camping at Valley Forge. The British were staying in Philadelphia. What might have happened if the British had attacked the Americans then?

_____

11. Which country decided to help the Americans at that time? What did this country have that America did not have?

_____

_____

_____

_____

12. Who was Deborah Sampson?

_____

_____

_____

_____

13. After the Americans had won their freedom, what did they have to do next?

_____

_____

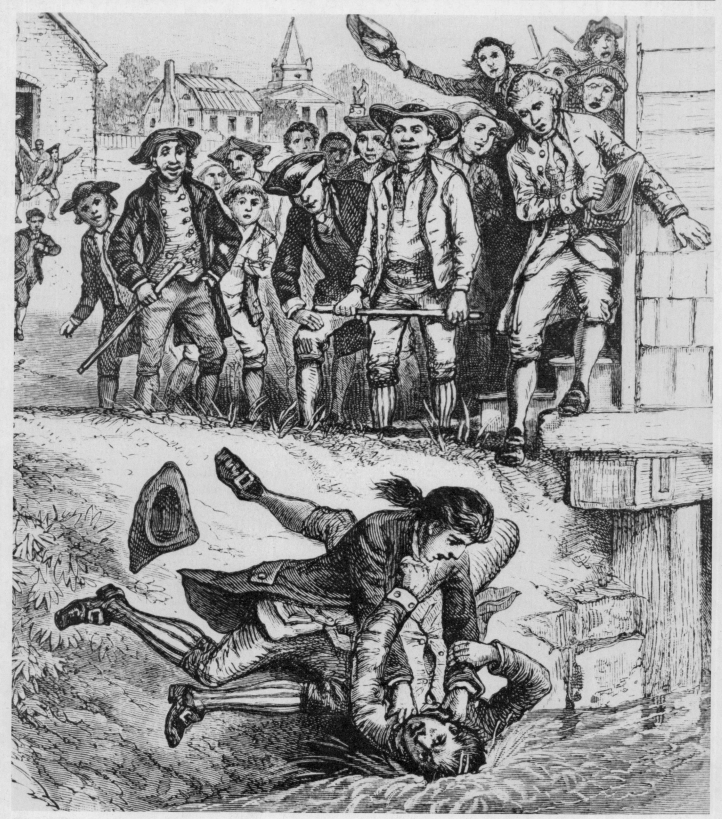

*Brawl between government supporter and rebel
at the time of Shays's Rebellion*

Chapter 4

A Government for the Ages

Words to Know

Articles of Confederation an agreement that set up the first government of the United States after the Revolution

compromise an agreement between two sides that is reached when each side gives up part of its demands

Constitution the law and plan of the government of a country

discussion an exchange of ideas

federal relating to the central government (rather than to the governments of separate states)

horizon the line where the sky meets the earth or the sea

levy to require; to collect

pardoned freed from punishment

population the number of people living in a place

rebellion a fight against the government or against another group or person in power

The two men stood eye to eye, looking angrily at each other. The taller one, lean and hard, was wearing worn and dirty clothes. The shorter one was dressed in a clean uniform.

"Mr. Shays," the shorter man said, "this army post is owned by the government of the United States of America. I order you to leave it!"

"What government? There is no government that I can see. What you call a government can't protect the farmers of this country from having their farms stolen. If this is what you call a government, give me back the British!"

"I will not hear it! Take your men and leave!"

"Who will make us leave?" Shays asked. "The United States government? Don't make me laugh!"

"The state of Massachusetts will do it."

"General Shepard, for six years I fought for the state of Massachusetts and for our country. I fought under General Washington, as did many of the men here. Now your courts are taking away our farms. Is this the thanks we get?"

"I have no choice. Leave now, or we will drive you out."

"We will not leave until you promise us we can keep our farms!"

The small man turned and walked back to his troops. An officer greeted him. "How did it go, General?"

General Shepard looked grim. "Captain, fire some cannon shots into the mob."

"Our Government Does Not Work!"

The cannon shots broke up what we now call "Shays's Rebellion." But they also showed that the government that had been set up after the Revolution did not work.

Shays's Rebellion started when many Massachusetts farmers could not pay the tax the state had placed on them. They were already in debt and were getting little money for their crops. The courts in Massachusetts had begun taking away the farms of those who would not pay. Shays and his group of farmers shut down the courts in order to put a stop to this.

Shays also made plans to attack an army post to get guns. The United States government knew about this. But because it had no army at that time, it could not stop him. The **federal** government asked the government of Massachusetts to step in. But Massachusetts didn't have an army, either. Nor did it have the cash to raise one. The soldiers who finally put down the farmers' revolt were hired by Massachusetts businessmen. Shays and some other leaders were caught and sentenced to die. However, they were later **pardoned.**

The rebellion gave the country a shock. George Washington wrote, "If the government can not protect its own posts from a group of farmers, how can our country protect itself from powerful foreign countries?"

Why was the American government so weak? First we must understand that the government of 1786 was not the one we have today. It had been drawn up in the last days of the Revolution under an agreement known as the **Articles of Confederation.** There was no president to lead the country and carry out the laws. There was no Supreme Court to settle important arguments. The government was run by Congress, and Congress was run by the states. Each state had one vote. Before Congress could pass any act, nine states had to agree to it.

Even before Shays's Rebellion, it was clear that the new government did not work well. It was hard to get the states to agree on anything. And when Congress did something a state did not like, the state could—and did—simply ignore it.

In many ways, the states looked upon themselves as separate countries. There was no single unified American spirit. Citizens were more loyal to the states they lived in than to the nation as a whole.

Also, Congress did not yet have the power to **levy** taxes. The government had no way of getting money to pay for the things it needed—such as an army.

Many American leaders believed that something had to be done quickly. They feared that if the government was not made stronger, there soon would be no United States at all.

Meeting in Philadelphia

During the last days of Shays's Rebellion, 55 men came together in Philadelphia to discuss ways to strengthen the government. They had been sent by 12 of the 13 states. Rhode Island, the smallest state, felt that any change would leave it with less power. Therefore, Rhode Island refused to send anyone.

Among those who went to the meeting were three very famous men. George Washington, tall and broad-shouldered, arrived in Philadelphia wearing his old army uniform. He was deeply respected by Americans everywhere. After Washington, Benjamin Franklin was the most famous citizen in the United States. A scientist, writer, and statesman, he was thought of as being both wise and witty. Now, at the age of 81, Franklin was performing his last act of public service. The third of our famous people was James Madison. Highly respected for his quick mind, Madison felt strongly about the need for a more powerful central government. For his work at the meeting, he would become known as the "father of the **Constitution**."

James Madison

Big States Versus Small States

The delegates met in Philadelphia in May of 1787. On the first day, they agreed on everything that came before them. They all felt that George Washington should run the meeting. This was a perfect choice, for Washington was respected by everyone there. He did not speak often, but when he did, the delegates paid close attention. The delegates also agreed that, in spite of the summer heat, they would lock the doors and close the windows and curtains. This would keep the **discussions** secret until the new plan was completed.

The first day, however, was the only one on which the delegates were of one mind. After that, they agreed on almost nothing. They argued throughout the summer and into the early part of the fall. Their most important question had to do with the number of votes each state could cast. Would all the states have an equal say? Or would the states with more people have more votes?

The delegates from Virginia put forward a plan that gave more power to the large states than to the small states. It called for each state to have votes in Congress according to its **population.** The states that had the most people would have the most representatives. The large states liked this idea. And the small states hated it. William Patterson, the delegate from New Jersey, said, "Under this plan, Virginia would have 16 votes, but Georgia will have only one. The large states will control everything. We will be swallowed up."

The small states presented a plan giving each state, regardless of size, only one vote. James Wilson, a delegate from Pennsylvania, answered for the large states. "The same numbers of people should have the same numbers of votes. Different numbers of people should have different numbers of votes. Pennsylvania will not accept any other plan."

The argument went on for six weeks. It seemed that neither side would give in. At this point, the meeting might have fallen apart. Fortunately, a Connecticut delegate named Roger Sherman found a middle ground.

"Why not have two houses of Congress?" he said. "In one house, all states will have the same number of votes. In the other house, the number will depend on the number of people in the state."

This would protect both the large and the small states. It didn't take long for all the delegates to go along with the idea. Sherman's plan was accepted on July 16.

For three long months, the delegates argued about other parts of the government. Many times they seemed unable to reach agreement. But each time they managed to work out a **compromise.** Finally they had their new plan. It was written down as the Constitution of the United States of America. Thirty-nine of the 55 delegates signed it.

Over the next few months, people in the 13 states discussed the new plan. One by one, the states approved the Constitution. Although it has changed some over the years, this is the basic set of laws we still follow today. It has helped a weak collection of 13 separate states become a strong country of 50 unified states.

During the long debates over the Constitution, Benjamin Franklin had sat quietly, listening to the delegates speak. Often he had looked at the tall chair in which George Washington sat. He had noticed that the back of the chair was carved with a large sun just above the **horizon.** Was it a rising sun or a setting sun? Franklin could not decide.

On the last day of the meeting, Franklin rose to speak. "This Constitution that we are about to sign will surprise our enemies. They are waiting for us to break up. They think we plan only to cut each other's throat."

Then Franklin pointed to Washington's chair. "For many weeks I have looked at that sun behind Mr. Washington without being able to tell whether it was a rising sun or a setting sun. But now, seeing this Constitution we have before us, I am happy to know that it is a rising sun."

Franklin was right. And on April 6, 1789, Congress elected George Washington to be the first president of the United States. America was seeing the light of a new day. It would be a time of growth, strength, and freedom.

The Sun Rising Over America

Benjamin Franklin

EXERCISE 4

Match each statement on the left with the person on the right who might have written or said it.

1. _____ "The large states will control everything. We will be swallowed up."

2. _____ "I fought for the state of Massachusetts and for our country. I fought for General Washington, as did many of the men here. Now your courts are taking away our farms."

3. _____ "Why not have two houses of Congress? In one house, all states will have the same number of votes. In the other house, the number will depend on the number of people in the state."

4. _____ "Different numbers of people should have different numbers of votes."

5. _____ "But, seeing this Constitution we have before us, I am happy to know that it is a rising sun."

6. _____ "If the government can not protect its own posts from a group of farmers, how can our country protect itself from powerful foreign countries?"

a. Daniel Shays

b. George Washington

c. Benjamin Franklin

d. Roger Sherman

e. James Wilson

f. William Patterson

Decide whether the following statements are true or false. Write T beside those that are true and F beside those that are false.

7. _____ Shays's Rebellion took place in the state of Pennsylvania.

8. _____ Shays's Rebellion was led by a farmer.

9. _____ Daniel Shays and other leaders of this revolt were sentenced and hanged.

10. _____ General Shepard was a member of the British army.

11. _____ The Articles of Confederation had been drawn up at the beginning of the Revolutionary War.

12. _____ In 1786, there was a Congress, but there was no Supreme Court.

13. _____ When Congress did something the states didn't like, the states almost always agreed to follow and obey Congress.

14. _____ In May of 1787, 12 of the 13 states met in Philadelphia to form a stronger government.

15. _____ Their most important question had to do with the power each state would have in the new government.

16. _____ The "father of the Constitution" was Benjamin Franklin.

17. _____ The Constitution is the basic set of laws we still follow today.

18. _____ In 1789, George Washington was chosen by Congress to be the first President of the United States.

Crossing the Great Plains

Chapter 5

To the West

Words to Know

continent a large mass of land; North America is one of the earth's seven continents

frontier land that has just been settled and is near other land that is not settled

transportation the moving of goods and people from one place to another

In 1804, President Thomas Jefferson had told Meriwether Lewis that the trip west would be hard. But Lewis had never thought he might lose his life crossing the **continent.**

For more than a year, Meriwether Lewis, William Clark, and 45 other men had traveled through freezing cold, snow, and heavy rains. On the eastern slope of the Rocky Mountains, they had met a Shoshone Indian woman named Sacajawea. She had not lived in Shoshone country for many years. However, she remembered it very well and offered to lead the party across the mountains.

Six months later, just when the trip should have been getting easier, Lewis and Clark faced a most dangerous moment. Coming toward them was a large group of Shoshone Indians wearing war paint and carrying weapons. It was clear that they were angry.

Lewis and Clark had hoped to buy horses from the Shoshone. But the Indians wanted Lewis and Clark to turn back. They knew what had happened to other Indians when the white people came. The Native Americans had lost their land and their way of life.

A tall Shoshone chief spoke to Lewis.

"You have a Shoshone woman with you?"

Lewis said he had. He wondered if the Shoshone would be angry at this. Sacajawea started walking toward the chief. Then she stopped and smiled.

"Hello, my brother," she said.

For a long moment, the Shoshone stared in surprise at Sacajawea. Then his mouth opened into a wide smile. "So, sister, you have returned."

"Yes, I have."

"And these men?"

"They are my friends. They only want horses."

"We will give them what they want and send them on their way."

From Sea to Shining Sea

So Lewis and Clark passed through Shoshone country on their way to the Pacific Ocean. They became the first known white Americans to make this overland journey. Upon returning, they gave President Jefferson much valuable information about the people, plants, and animals of the West.

Lewis and Clark made their trip because the country was reaching out to the West and needed to know more about it. In 1803, the United States had bought the large Louisiana Territory from France. The "Louisiana Purchase," as it was called, doubled the size of the country. After Lewis and Clark's journey, small numbers of settlers began pushing into this land.

"Going west," they called it. Americans had been doing it long before Lewis and Clark. When land along the East Coast became crowded, people had packed up their belongings and traveled to the **frontier**. After the Revolution, "going west" meant crossing the Appalachian Mountains into Kentucky, Tennessee, and Ohio. These areas all had enough people by 1803 to have become states. From 1816 to 1821, the United States added a new state every year. By 1821, there were 24 states, 11 of them in "the West."

In 1846, war broke out between the United States and Mexico over the question of who owned Texas. The fighting lasted 16 months. When Mexico was defeated, the United States gained not only Texas, but most of the land in Arizona, California, Nevada, New Mexico, and Utah. In 1850, California became the 31st state. The country then stretched from coast to coast.

Sacajawea and Meriwether Lewis

Pioneer Life

Nearly everyone in the West lived on a farm, and farm families worked long and hard hours. They had settled in a land with thick forests. Their first job was to clear the land of trees and pull out the stumps. For months, a family might live under a piece of cloth tied to the trees. Thomas and Nancy Lincoln, for example, moved to Indiana with their nine-year-old son Abraham in December of 1816. Through the long winter, the family lived in an open shelter of logs and cloth. They were able to stay alive only by keeping a fire going at all times.

After the land was cleared, a family would put up a log cabin. Inside, it was likely to be dark, dusty, and crowded. Cold air blew through the walls. When it rained, the dirt floor turned to mud. The deerskins covering the windows let in little light. The single room in the cabin served as bedroom, kitchen, living room, and dining room.

There was always plenty of work to do. The family planted crops in the fields and hunted and collected firewood in the forests. Often people kept a few pigs. And there was usually something to prepare in the kitchen. There were almost no stores. If people needed a broom, a rake, or some other tool, they either had to make it or trade for it. They spent their evenings making soap, candles, cloth, shoes, and tools.

Life on the frontier could be lonely. So the families got together for long parties. At these parties, people played as hard as they had worked. The square dancing, wrestling matches, eating, drinking, and singing went on through the day and night.

Getting There

How did families go west? There were few roads, and most of them were in terrible shape. In dry weather, the dust was so thick it coated travelers' bodies. In wet weather, the roads would become rivers of mud. When a horse or wagon got stuck, it could take all day to get it out.

If America was going to settle its West, it needed easier ways to get there. In 1811, the American government started building the National Road westward from Maryland. Every few years, a new section was opened. By the 1830s, the road reached almost to the Mississippi River. Thousands of people used it to get to the places where they hoped to start new lives.

As the settlement of the West continued, the farmers faced a new problem. Though they could raise large crops, there was no one to buy them. The big markets were in the cities of the East. How were the farmers to get the crops east? Not by river, since the rivers ran south or west. Not by road, since the trip was so long that the crops might rot.

One answer was to build canals. The Erie Canal was the longest and best known. It stretched all the way from Lake Erie to the Hudson River. It was then an easy trip downriver to New York City. When the canal was finished in 1825, it proved to be the best way to move crops from the farms to the cities. It also carried factory goods and thousands of new settlers from east to west.

Still, canals were not the perfect means of **transportation.** Though travel by canal was faster than by road, at five miles per hour it was still quite slow. In winter, when the canals filled with ice, it was even slower. Most importantly, the canals could not go over the mountains. What was the answer to the transportation problem? How was a growing country to get its people, crops, and goods from one place to another?

Horse Versus Train

Two coaches stood side by side on bright shining rails. One was hitched to a strong young horse. The other was attached to a strange-looking steam boiler. Black smoke puffed noisily from the boiler's smokestack. The words "Tom Thumb" were written on the side of this "iron horse."

On this day in April, 1830, a man named Peter Cooper crawled over the Tom Thumb, making sure that everything was in order. Off to the side, a group of men in expensive black clothing watched with interest.

When all was ready, a signal was given and the race began. At first, the horse pulled far ahead. But slowly—ever so slowly—the Tom Thumb started to close the gap. Then the Tom Thumb came up even with the horse-drawn coach. The horse ran as fast as it could, but the Tom Thumb pulled ahead. It was far in the lead when suddenly there was a loud pop. The Tom Thumb slowed down and rolled to a stop. Peter Cooper watched unhappily as the horse-drawn coach overtook the Tom Thumb and rode off into the distance.

Cooper's steam-powered train had failed its first test. However, the day was not lost. The men watching were the owners of the new Baltimore and Ohio Railroad. Until now, all their coaches had been pulled over the rails by horses. Yet they had seen enough of the Tom Thumb to know where the future lay. On the spot, they ordered two steam engines from Peter Cooper. The age of the railroad had begun.

It now seemed that an answer had been found to America's transportation problem. Railroad trains ran in almost any weather. They were much faster than canal boats. And the trains could go wherever tracks could be put down, even along the sides of mountains.

Peter Cooper

By the 1840s, "railroad fever" was sweeping the country. By the 1850s, Cleveland, Detroit, Chicago, and St. Louis were linked by rail to the East.

In the 1790s, there had been only 4 million people in the whole of the United States. Almost everyone lived within 250 miles of the Atlantic Ocean. Fifty years later, twice that number of people lived in just the states west of the Appalachians.

It was an exciting time. People took whatever they could carry, sold what they couldn't, and headed west. An Englishman visiting America in 1830 found the roads, rails, and canals filled with travelers. "Rich ones, poor ones, old or young, single people, large families—all are on the move," he wrote. "Old America seems to be breaking up. Everyone is moving west."

EXERCISE 5

Study the chart below. Then answer the questions that follow.

1791	Vermont became a state.
1792	Kentucky became a state.
1803	The United States bought the Louisiana Territory. Ohio became a state.
1804	Lewis and Clark began their trip.
1806	Lewis and Clark returned to Washington, D.C.
1811	Workers started building the National Road.
1821	Missouri became a state.
1825	The Erie Canal was finished.
1828	The Baltimore and Ohio Railroad began.
1830	The Baltimore and Ohio Railroad bought two steam engines from Peter Cooper.
1850	California became a state.
1860	There were 30,000 miles of railroad in the U.S.

1. Which state joined the United States the same year that the United States bought the Louisiana Territory?

   _____

2. How long did the Lewis and Clark trip last?

   _____

3. When did the United States start building a road that reached from Maryland almost to the Mississippi River?

   _____

4. How many years after the Baltimore and Ohio Railroad started did it buy steam engines from Peter Cooper?

   _____

5. In what year did the United States get a state that touches the Pacific Ocean?

   _____

In the spaces below, write the word or words that best complete these statements.

6. Lewis and Clark were led across the Rocky Mountains by a Shoshone Indian woman named _____ .

7. Their journey took place while _____ was president.

8. Lewis and Clark had made their trip because _____
_____
_____ .

9. The size of the United States was doubled when it bought the Louisiana Territory from _____ .

10. Settlers in the West lived mostly on _____ .

11. Because there were few stores there, when people in the West needed new tools they had to _____
_____ .

12. The roads that people took to get to the West were often in poor shape. In dry weather, they could be filled with _____ . In wet weather, they could be filled with _____ .

13. In 1825, the best way to move crops from farms in the West to cities in the East was on the _____ Canal.

14. One problem with canals was that they filled with ice in the winter. Also, the canals could not _____ .

15. The steam engine that Peter Cooper became known for was called the _____ .
Before it was built, trains were pulled by _____ .

16. In the 1790s, most people in the United States lived within 250 miles of the _____ .

Chapter 6

The Age of Jackson

Words to Know

citizens   members of a country, state, or city

democracy   a form of government in which power comes from and belongs to the people

frontiersmen   people living on the frontier

immigrants   people who leave their homelands to live in another place

inauguration   the swearing in of a president

industry   the making of goods on a large scale, such as in a factory

property   things that are owned by people

self-evident   clearly true

slavery   the "owning" of another person, who is treated like a piece of property

urban   of or relating to a city

It was March 24, 1829. Washington, D.C., had never seen anything like this. The city was filled with excitement. It was **Inauguration** Day. Andrew Jackson was being sworn in as the seventh president of the United States.

Thousands of people watched as Jackson took office. Later, they crowded around him, trying to shake his hand. Most of these toughened men were from the frontier. Their clothes were made of animal skins. They chewed big plugs of tobacco.

At a party in the White House, the **frontiersmen** stood on fancy velvet chairs to get a view of their hero. Others pushed to the tables to get something to eat. Food and drink spilled on the beautiful carpet. Some rooms were so crowded that people climbed out the windows in order to leave the White House.

Off in a corner, Senator Daniel Webster looked on unhappily. In a letter to a friend, he later wrote, "There are thousands of frontier people in the city. I never saw anything like it before. Some of them have come 500 miles to see Jackson. They look on us, the people of wealth and power, as the enemy. They think Jackson will save the country from us!"

A Hero to the People

Who was Jackson, and why were people so excited about him? Andrew Jackson was very different from anyone who'd been president before him. Some earlier presidents, such as George Washington, had come from very rich families. Others, like John Adams, had had very good educations. And some, like Thomas Jefferson, were both rich and well educated. In addition, all the presidents before Jackson had come from either Virginia or Massachusetts.

Andrew Jackson, like most Americans, was born very poor. Yet he had grown up to become very rich and to be elected president. That made him a hero. He proved that a poor person born in a log cabin could rise to power in the United States. In most other countries, that could never have happened.

The log cabin where Andrew Jackson was born was in North Carolina. His mother and father had both died by the time he was 14. As a boy, he was too poor to go to school for very long. Mostly, he taught himself.

Jackson moved to Tennessee and became a lawyer. As one of the first lawyers in that state, he became quite wealthy. He was elected to Congress, and later the voters made him a judge. But no matter how high he rose, Andrew Jackson remained a man of the frontier. People called him the toughest, bravest, hardest-working man in the state.

Growing Cities

That Andrew Jackson was president showed how America was changing. As the country spread out, Westerners wanted to have one of their own as president. But it wasn't only the frontier that was behind Andrew Jackson. He was also a hero to the workers in America's cities. And as the country grew, it had more and more **urban** laborers and fewer farmers.

In 1800, when Thomas Jefferson had been elected president, the United States was a nation of farmers. Only 6 out of every 100 Americans lived in the cities at that time. But by 1828, when Jackson was elected, the United States was slowly changing into a nation of city people.

Why did people go to the cities? They went because that was where most of the jobs were. Rich people were building factories in the Northeast, and many workers were needed. Large numbers of people in states such as Pennsylvania, New York, and Massachusetts left the farms to work in factories. By 1845, the year that Andrew Jackson died, more than 20 out of every 100 Americans lived in cities.

Many of these people had been born in the countries of Europe. As American **industry** grew, more and more people were drawn to the United States. Often the **immigrants** came in order to escape terrible living conditions. In the early 1800s, many European farmers had trouble growing enough food to feed their families. This "Great Hunger" drove people to come to the United States. Most of these immigrants were forced to work at low-paying jobs and to live in run-down buildings. Still, a low-paying job was better than no job at all. And in America, people had rights they did not have in Europe. The most important of these was the right to vote. The **citizens** could choose who they wanted to look after their interests. This was something new, even for America.

Horace Mann, the "father of American public education"

When the Constitution was approved in 1787, many of our leaders did not believe that poor Americans would use their votes wisely. In the nation's early years, only white men who owned **property** could vote. Poor white men and all women, Indians, and blacks had no say in the government. As the United States grew, more people were allowed a voice. By 1828, when Jackson was elected president, almost all white men in the United States were permitted to vote.

Some people were frightened by this. They believed that only rich, educated white males knew enough to run things. Many of those with money feared that poor people would elect leaders who would steal their wealth and ruin the country.

The poor saw things differently. By getting the vote, they were able to elect leaders who would work for them. These leaders were able to pass laws to deal with some of the problems that had arisen as America grew.

In the early 1800s, progress came about in several areas. Many states passed laws that set up free public schools for both boys and girls. Before this, the schools were expensive

"They'll Ruin the Country"

Dorothea Dix, whose work led to great improvements in the care of the mentally ill

and open only to boys. Now there were states that even set up schools for blind people. In some places, state hospitals were built for the mentally ill.

We shouldn't get the idea, however, that the United States was a perfect **democracy.** Some Americans—Indians and blacks—hardly had any rights at all. American women, besides not being allowed to vote, were not allowed to own property. And if they earned money at a job, they had to give it to their husbands.

All Men and Women Are Equal

On a warm day in July of 1848, a crowd of 100 men and women gathered outside a church in Seneca Falls, New York. They had been drawn to the church by a notice placed in a newspaper:

WOMEN'S RIGHTS MEETING!

The meeting was the idea of Elizabeth Cady Stanton and Lucretia Mott. For many years, they had talked with each other about equal rights for American women. Now, they decided, the time had come to do something about it.

When the people tried to get into the church, they found that someone had locked all the doors. A small boy climbed through an open window. Within minutes, the church doors were opened and the meeting began. Elizabeth Cady Stanton spoke first. The beginning of her talk sounded like the Declaration of Independence. But there was a difference. The Declaration of Independence says, "We hold these truths to be **self-evident:** that all men are created equal." Stanton's report says, "We hold these truths to be self-evident: that all men and women are created equal."

Stanton went on to demand that women be given the right to vote. The audience was moved by her call. They cheered and cheered. Then they voted to approve the report. However, in 1848 the United States was not yet ready to give women the right to vote. It would take another 70 years for that to happen.

If so many people did not have rights, what made the Age of Jackson special? After all, there was still **slavery** in America in the early 1800s. And no country that allowed this to exist could really call itself a democracy. So why do we consider this a great time for democracy?

Elizabeth Cady Stanton

We should remember that democracy in America did not come about overnight. It took many years and the work of many Americans. When Anne Hutchinson left the Massachusetts Bay Colony, she took a step forward for democracy. When William Penn founded Pennsylvania for people of all backgrounds, he took another step. The Declaration of Independence was a giant step forward. Giving the vote to poor white men was a step. Today we sometimes take our ideas about freedom and democracy for granted. But they weren't taken for granted in Jackson's time. Americans were testing the ideas then. They showed the world that these ideas could work.

EXERCISE 6

Complete each statement below. Write the letter of the word or words that make it correct.

a. Congress

b. immigrants

c. urban laborers

d. democracy

e. lawyer

f. property

g. evident

h. farmers

i. Elizabeth Cady Stanton

j. frontier

k. judge

l. public schools

m. Daniel Webster

n. New York

o. the Great Hunger

p. jobs

q. Tennessee

r. vote

1. When something is obvious, it is self- _____ .

2. When the power to run a country comes from the people, their government is called a _____ .

3. Andrew Jackson was different from the presidents who were elected before him because he came from the _____ .

4. Senator _____ watched Jackson's inauguration unhappily because he thought poor people considered him an enemy.

5. As a young man, Jackson moved to the state of _____ .

6. Jackson became a _____ , a member of _____ , and a _____ before he was elected president.

7. During the Age of Jackson, America was changing from a nation of _____ to a nation of _____ .

8. People moved to the cities because that's where the most _____ were.

9. Rich people were building factories in Jackson's time in states such as _____ .

10. People who come to the United States from other countries are known as _____ .

11. One reason people came to the United States was so that they could _____ for their leaders.

12. In the early 1800s, many people in Europe had trouble growing enough food to eat. This time is known as _____ .

13. When the Constitution was approved in 1787, many states had rules allowing only people who owned _____ to vote.

14. Laws passed during the Age of Jackson set up free _____ .

15. At the Seneca Falls meeting in 1848, _____ read a report that sounded like the Declaration of Independence but that contained important differences.

Chapter 7

Slavery

Words to Know

armory   a place where guns and other arms are stored

business   the buying and selling of goods and services

capitol   the building where a state or national government meets (a capital is the city or town where the government is located)

confederate   joined together; the Southern side in the Civil War was called the Confederacy

denounce   to speak against

mansion   a very large and fancy house

plantation   a large farm where crops are cared for by workers who live there

secede   to withdraw from the rest of a country in order to form a new one; the South seceded from the United States in 1860

It was four o'clock in the morning. At the **plantation** of James Rutherford, a horn sounded loudly. In the Rutherford **mansion,** the family members heard the horn, turned over, and went back to sleep. But near the mansion, in small, dirty wooden cabins, people were slowly rising from the straw mats on which they had been sleeping. They dressed quietly in the darkness and headed out to the cotton fields. For the slaves of the Rutherford plantation, another day had begun.

Gabriel Prosser was one of those slaves. He was 19 and had been born on the Rutherford plantation. He expected to die there. Six days a week, for 52 weeks of the year, he got up at four in the morning to work in the fields. Prosser would probably have to do the same thing for the rest of his life. It was against the law to teach a slave skills such as reading and writing.

Gabriel Prosser was "lucky"—he had never been beaten. But he knew that on many plantations, slaves were beaten for talking back or for not working quite as hard as the owners demanded.

Prosser's parents lived with him on the plantation. His father, who had a heart problem, worked in the Rutherford mansion. His mother worked in the fields. Though Prosser had a brother and a sister, he no longer saw them. Two years earlier, Rutherford did not have the money to buy seed. So he chose a group of young slaves, took them into town, and sold them. Prosser's brother and sister were in that group. His parents cried when their children were sold. His father begged Rutherford to stop the sale, but the owner just shrugged his shoulders and said there was nothing he could do. He needed the money, he said. Otherwise, he could plant no crop that year.

This was slavery, an evil system that was a way of life in parts of the South. It wasted people's talents, destroyed their health, and led to early deaths. But Southern whites came to believe that the South could not survive without slavery. They also came to believe that other Americans would stop at nothing to end slavery. At that point, white Southerners took steps to break up the United States. They almost succeeded. The Civil War, which followed, was one of the bloodiest in American history.

The strange thing was that slavery had almost died out 75 years before the Civil War. Slavery grew in importance when large numbers of people were needed to work the South's cotton plantations. But in the last part of the 1700s, cotton had become less important. The crop wore out the soil. If it was grown in the same spot for too many years, that land could not be farmed. Also, cotton was not worth anything until the seeds were separated from the fuzz that grew around them. This took a lot of time and made the cotton very expensive. By the 1790s, many cotton farmers were turning to other crops.

Then, in 1793, a little black box saved cotton—and slavery.

That box was the cotton gin. It was a machine that separated the seeds from the fuzz much faster than any person could do it. With the gin, farmers could again make money growing cotton. It once again became the South's most important crop, in new areas as well as old.

As "King Cotton" spread, so did slavery. Louisiana, Mississippi, Alabama, Florida, and Texas joined the Union as "slave states." In these states, slavery was allowed by law. By 1850, slaves made up nearly one third of the people in the South.

Slavery was tightly controlled. But there were times when those who were held down by it fought back.

"Cotton Is King"

Eli Whitney, inventor of the cotton gin

"I Have Nothing More to Offer"

Gabriel Prosser walked through the streets of Richmond, noting the city's important buildings. He saw the state **capitol** and the **armory.** For weeks, Prosser had been looking over the city. He also had been speaking to fellow slaves in the surrounding area, urging them to rise up against their masters. He had managed to put together a small force of slaves who were ready to follow him.

Prosser's plan called for the capture of Richmond. Then the nearby towns would be taken. When Virginia was under control, all slaves would be freed.

But the revolt never took place. Prosser was betrayed. Also, as his forces were gathering, a violent rainstorm washed out the roads and bridges leading into Richmond.

Prosser was arrested. He did not deny his plans. He was quickly brought to trial and sentenced to die. Before he and 36 others were hanged, in August of 1800, Prosser made a powerful speech. "I have nothing more to offer than George Washington would have had to offer had he been taken by the British and put to trial by them." Gabriel Prosser gave his life in the hope that others might have freedom.

There were other slave rebellions throughout the early 1800s. Though they all failed, they revealed the hatred of the system that kept people in chains.

The abolitionists, who were mostly Northerners, wanted to end (abolish) slavery. Black and white, they went around the country **denouncing** it. Many abolitionists did more than just talk about slavery. Sometimes they put their lives in great danger by helping slaves to escape. Unfortunately, not everyone in the North was against slavery; it had been accepted as a normal part of American life. The abolitionists were attacked in both the North and the South.

Harriet Tubman

It was a warm summer night in 1851. All seemed quiet on the plantation. Outside the slave cabins, a woman sang a song called "Steal Away." The men, women, and children in the cabins heard the song. They knew it was a signal to wrap the few things they owned and make their escape.

The woman singing the song was Harriet Tubman. Born a slave, she had escaped to the North, promising to return one day to help others. She more than made good on her promise. Harriet Tubman went back to slave country 20 times. She helped lead more than 300 black people to freedom. Slave catchers tried hard to take her, but they were never able to. She always managed to get away.

The Underground Railroad

Harriet Tubman was a conductor on the Underground Railroad. This was not really a railroad, and it was not underground. Rather, it was a secret means of escape for slaves. Abolitionists set up "stations"—places of safety—along the different routes. There the slaves, called "passengers," could hide. Brave people called "conductors" helped lead the slaves to the North. About 50,000 slaves escaped to freedom along the Underground Railroad.

Two Ways of Life

While slavery grew stronger in the South, very different ways of life developed in other parts of the country. The North became a center for industry. Its population had increased rapidly as people moved there to work in the mills and factories.

As a result, the North did not have a great need for slaves. Though there had been some slavery there since colonial times, it had mostly died out. By the early years of the 1800s, all the Northern states had outlawed slavery.

The North and the South had very different ideas about how the government should be run. The North wanted a strong central government. The South wanted each state to have more of its own power. And on both sides, those who were wealthy felt that the other side was a threat to their way of doing **business.**

Both the North and the South had a strong interest in the West, which was fast becoming an important area for farming and ranching. Northerners and Southerners realized that someday the western lands would become states in the Union. Would they be free or slave? The answer was important because every state had votes in Congress. Those votes could be cast either for or against slavery.

As each Western territory asked to become a state, arguments raged all over the land. In 1858, a man in Illinois who was running for the United States Senate took note of this when he said, "A house divided against itself cannot stand. I believe our country cannot last half slave and half free."

Abraham Lincoln did not win that election. But his words made him known in all parts of the country. In the North, people looked to him to hold the United States together and to keep slavery from spreading to the West. In the South, people saw him as a dangerous enemy of slavery and of the South itself. Many Southerners said they would **secede** if Lincoln became president.

The First Shots

Jefferson Davis

In 1860, Abraham Lincoln did become president of the United States. Shortly after the election, seven Southern states announced they were no longer a part of the United States. In February of 1861, leaders of these states met to form their own country. They elected Jefferson Davis president of the **Confederate** States of America. Four more states soon joined the Confederacy. Tension mounted. Lincoln felt he could not permit the South to secede. War seemed impossible to avoid.

It began at Fort Sumter, which is located on an island in the harbor of Charleston, South Carolina. The South had already left the Union, but this fort remained under Northern control. The Southern forces had gathered across the water and were waiting for the signal to attack. On April 12, the Southern cannons began firing. All day, they pounded the fort. Finally, Fort Sumter surrendered. Southerners took control and raised the flag of the Confederacy. The Civil War had started. It would not end until four terrible years had passed and hundreds of thousands of lives had been lost.

Battle of Fort Sumter

EXERCISE 7

Fill in the circle beside the words that best complete each of the following statements.

1. Slavery almost died out in the late 1700s because
   ⓐ cotton growing had become too expensive.
   ⓑ the Southern states outlawed it.
   ⓒ the government ordered Southerners to free their slaves.

2. Slavery was saved by the
   ⓐ invention of the cotton gin.
   ⓑ growing immigration from Europe.
   ⓒ support of the abolitionists.

3. When white Southerners said, "Cotton is king," they meant that it
   ⓐ was too important to the North.
   ⓑ caused too much trouble in the South.
   ⓒ was the South's most important crop.

4. The Underground Railroad was a system for
   ⓐ moving cotton to market.
   ⓑ helping slaves to escape.
   ⓒ moving soldiers around the South.

5. The West became important in the troubles between the North and the South because each side wondered if the Western states would
   ⓐ be free states or slave states.
   ⓑ join another country.
   ⓒ support slave rebellions.

6. Shortly after Abraham Lincoln was elected president,
   ⓐ the Underground Railroad began.
   ⓑ the Southern states seceded.
   ⓒ slavery was outlawed in the Nothern states.

Answer the questions below.

7. What was Gabriel Prosser's plan for a slave uprising?

   _____

   _____

   _____

8. Who were the abolitionists?

_____

_____

_____

9. Who was Harriet Tubman?

_____

_____

_____

10. How did the North and the South look differently at the role of the federal government?

_____

_____

_____

11. What did the North expect of Abraham Lincoln?

_____

_____

_____

12. How did the South see Lincoln?

_____

_____

_____

13. Who was elected president of the Confederate States of America?

_____

14. When and where was the first battle of the Civil War fought?

_____

_____

Battle of Bull Run

Chapter 8

The Civil War

Words to Know

amendment a formal change or addition

charity kindness

citation an award given for bravery or for service deserving praise

civilian one who is not a soldier

malice ill will; anger; hatred

prohibit to forbid; to prevent

secession the withdrawal of one part of a country from the rest of the country

surrender to give up

sympathy a feeling of pity

union a group of people tied together by a cause; the Northern side in the Civil War was called the Union

It was a bright sunny day in July of 1861. In Washington, D.C., smiling men and women climbed into horse-drawn carriages. They were carrying lunch boxes. They looked as though they were going to a picnic or sporting event.

But they were not off to lunch in the country or to a ball game. They were going to a battle. The citizens of Washington, D.C., were following the **Union** army as it marched down the road. At a stream called Bull Run, not far from the city, the Confederates were waiting. Washington had come out to watch the North win a victory that would end the South's rebellion.

There were some good reasons for the belief that the Union would quickly end the war. The North had a far larger population than the South. There were more people available to fight as soldiers, to work in the factories, and to grow food. The North had many more factories. It could make more guns and cannons. The North had many more miles of railroad, too. It could get soldiers, guns, cannons, and food to the front lines faster than the South could.

The war would be over soon. The South would be punished. Or so the people of Washington believed.

But it didn't turn out that way. At Bull Run, the North suffered a crushing defeat. The Southern army sent the Northerners fleeing back to Washington. The **civilians** and their wagons become part of the retreat. There was a great traffic jam as cannon fire roared overhead and people screamed at one another.

Finally, the citizens of Washington returned to their homes. It had been a very bad day. The news traveled quickly throughout the country. The South had won the first battle. People on both sides now saw that this would be a long, hard war.

Brother Against Brother

The smoke hung heavily after the battle of Shiloh. For two days in April, 1862, the armies had fought and killed. Thousands lay dead. A Northern general walked over the field and wondered how it could have come to this. Why did Americans have to spend years fighting and killing one another? The general passed a Northern soldier who was slowly and sadly digging a grave. The general nodded to the man in **sympathy**. The man must have been burying a friend. Then the general looked at the body the man was burying. The dead man was wearing the gray colors of the Confederacy. The general was surprised. "Private," the general asked, "with so many of our side dead, why do you bury this man?" Tears were running down the face of the soldier as he looked up at the general.

"Sir, this man here, I know he was a rebel. But, sir, he was also my brother. I must give him a decent resting place before I write my father."

When it was finally over, there was hardly a family in all the country that had not lost someone in the war. All wars are terrible. But the Civil War was terrible in a special way. It was not a war between different countries. A "civil" war is one which is fought between groups of people within the same country. The American Civil War caused families to be torn apart. It set cousin against cousin, brother against brother, and father against son.

Wounded Union soldiers

To defeat the South, the Union used what it called the 'Conda Plan. The South American snake called the anaconda kills by coiling itself around its prey and slowly squeezing the life out of it. In the same way, the North tried to use its army and navy to squeeze the South to death.

Since the South did not have many factories, it needed to trade its cotton for guns, cannons, and clothing. But Northern ships blockaded Southern harbors on the Atlantic and Gulf coasts and kept out goods from other countries. Also, the Northern army and navy captured towns along the Mississippi River, separating the western part of the Confederacy from the eastern part. This kept the South from moving armies and supplies from one part to the other. Finally, Northern armies set about destroying the roads, bridges, and railways in the South. Northern generals believed that the South could not hold out for long against this pressure.

But the best plans in the world cannot help an army if it does not have good leaders. And in the beginning, the Confederacy had far better leaders than the Union did. Generals such as Robert E. Lee and Stonewall Jackson outsmarted the Union generals. It was not until Lincoln named Ulysses S. Grant to lead the Northern armies that the Union started to get the upper hand.

Squeezing the South

Stonewall Jackson

Another problem for the North was that it did not always seem to know why it was fighting. Was the purpose of the war to end slavery? Was it to save the United States? Was it to allow for the growth of business?

Lincoln hated slavery and wanted to see it stopped. He had once said that, "If slavery isn't wrong, then nothing is wrong." But he had been afraid that if he put an end to slavery the country might break up. When the South seceded, Lincoln felt forced to go to war to keep the country whole. As the war went on, he saw that doing something to end slavery would encourage the North to fight better.

An End to Slavery

On January 1, 1863, Lincoln signed an order called the "Emancipation Proclamation." It **prohibited** slavery in all states still fighting the Union at that time. When he signed the order, Lincoln said, "I never in my life felt more certain that I was doing right than I do in signing this paper." The proclamation did not suddenly make anyone free. The South did not honor it, and it did not apply to all the states. Yet the proclamation helped lead to the passage of the Thirteenth **Amendment** to the Constitution. This legally abolished slavery throughout the country on December 18, 1865.

One part of the Emancipation Proclamation invited blacks to fight with the Northern forces. Many thousands signed up in the Union's army and navy. By the end of the war, more than 200,000 blacks had fought in some of the bloodiest battles of the war. Twenty black soldiers won America's highest **citation** for bravery, the Medal of Honor. About 38,000 black soldiers died in the fighting.

"With Malice Toward None. . . ."

Robert E. Lee

By early 1865, the 'Conda Plan had achieved its goals. The South lay in ruins. A Northern army had marched through Georgia and South Carolina destroying farms, railways, houses, sheds—anything that lay in its path. In Virginia, Grant's army had trapped Lee's forces. Lee now saw that the Southern cause was hopeless. At a small house in the town of Appomattox Court House on April 9, 1865, Lee **surrendered** his army to Grant. All over the North, people celebrated the end of the bloodshed.

But they did not celebrate for long. Five days after the war's end, Abraham Lincoln was shot and killed by a disturbed man named John Wilkes Booth. Booth, a supporter of the South, thought he was helping the South by this terrible act. What he had really done was kill the person who could best help the South recover. It had been Lincoln's great hope that he could bring the South back into the country as a full partner with the North. In the last days of the war, he had urged: "With **malice** toward none, with **charity** for all, let us work to bind up the nation's wounds."

Lincoln thought of the Southerners as Americans who had suffered greatly from a terrible war.

The Civil War was the most terrible war the United States has ever fought. It killed more than 600,000 people and left large parts of the South in ruins. It destroyed cities and farms. For many years to come, the United States would be torn by bitter hatreds that arose from the war.

Yet the war decided two important questions. Slavery and the threat of **secession** had troubled the United States almost since its founding. Never again would the law allow one person to own another as property. And never again would one state be able to have its way by removing itself from the nation. The United States had paid a great price with the Civil War. But it would become a stronger country. It would take its place as a leader among the nations of the world.

A Stronger Country

Abraham Lincoln

EXERCISE 8

Decide whether the following statements are true or false. Write T beside those that are true and F beside those that are false.

1. _____ Many people from Philadelphia went out to watch the battle of Bull Run, the first battle of the Civil War.

2. _____ Bull Run was a great success for the Northern forces.

3. _____ A war between different groups of people in the same country is known as a civil war.

4. _____ To defeat the South, the Union used its 'Conda Plan.

5. _____ By controlling the Hudson River, the Union split the Confederacy into a western and an eastern part.

6. _____ To prohibit something is to permit it to happen.

7. _____ Abraham Lincoln opposed slavery.

8. _____ At Appomattox Court House, Ulysses S. Grant surrendered his Southern army.

9. _____ Shortly after the war, Lincoln was shot and killed by John Wilkes Booth.

Answer the questions below.

10. At the beginning of the Civil War, the North thought it could quickly and easily beat the South. What three things did it have more of than the South?

_____

_____

_____

_____

11. In what way was the South better prepared to fight the war than the North was?

_____

_____

12. What were three different purposes the North sometimes seemed to have for fighting the war?

_____

_____

_____

_____

_____

13. Where did the Emancipation Proclamation prohibit slavery?

_____

_____

_____

14. What law prohibited slavery throughout the country?

_____

15. How many people died as a result of the Civil War?

_____

16. Which two questions did the Civil War decide?

_____

_____

_____

_____

Completion of the first transcontinental railroad

Chapter 9

The Last Frontier

It was one of the greatest races in American history. For six years, two railroad companies were busy laying track. They were working toward each other, one company heading west and the other east. The plan was to connect somewhere along the route. They crossed rivers, plains, and mountains. Each side was racing to put down the most track before they met. They were building America's first **transcontinental** railroad.

In December of 1863, while the Civil War was raging, the crews of the Central Pacific Railroad began working near Sacramento, California. Most of the workers were Chinese immigrants. They had made the long trip to America for the chance to earn a decent living.

For six years, they pushed east over mountain passes and deep **ravines.** Sometimes the workers had to hang out over the edges of cliffs to set dynamite. Sometimes they had to blast tunnels through solid rock.

While the Central Pacific laid track from the West, crews of the Union Pacific Railroad were working on America's Great Plains. They had started in Omaha, Nebraska. These workers were mostly American blacks and Irish and German immigrants. They pushed their way across the Plains and up through the high Rockies.

The crews worked from dawn to dusk. The work was so hard that each morning the men could hardly get themselves up to begin a new day's work. But somehow they did, day after day. In the summer, many fainted from the heat. In the winter, many died from the cold.

The heat and the cold were not their only concerns. As the railroads crossed the country, they cut through the hunting grounds of many Indian tribes. Angry Indians began attacking railroad crews and supply trains.

Leland Stanford

The work did not stop. On May 10, 1869, the two groups met at a place in Utah called Promontory Point. While a **photographer** clicked away and workers looked on, a tall, well-dressed man stepped forward. He was Leland Stanford, president of the Central Pacific Railroad. In his hands he held a large sledge hammer. At his feet was a spike of solid gold. The spike would hold in place the last two sections of rail—one put down by a Union Pacific crew, the other by a Central Pacific crew.

Leland Stanford swung once—and missed. The workers on both sides roared with laughter. He swung again and tapped the spike into the ground. Other officials finished the job. Then the message was flashed over the **telegraph** lines: "From the Atlantic to the Pacific, the country is linked by rail." Americans had waited for many years to hear that.

In San Francisco, people held parades and fired rockets into the evening sky. In Philadelphia, the bell at Independence Hall was rung. In Chicago, a seven-mile-long parade marched throughout the night.

Settling In

In Chapter 5, we learned how Americans had long been moving to the West. But it wasn't until after the Civil War that large numbers of them began settling in the lands between the Mississippi River and the Rocky Mountains. This large **prairie,** known as the Great Plains, became the last frontier.

By the 1890s, five rail lines ran across the Great Plains to the West Coast. Hundreds of towns sprang up along their paths. The land between the Mississippi and the Rockies became filled with farmers, ranchers, and townspeople. Beef cattle were brought to the cattle towns, and crops were brought to the farm towns. From there they were shipped east.

In the 250 years between 1620 and 1870, Americans had settled about 400 million acres of land. In the 30 years between 1870 and 1900, another 400 million acres were settled. The central and western prairies and woodlands were "tamed" with the machines of the East. By 1900, the last frontier had disappeared.

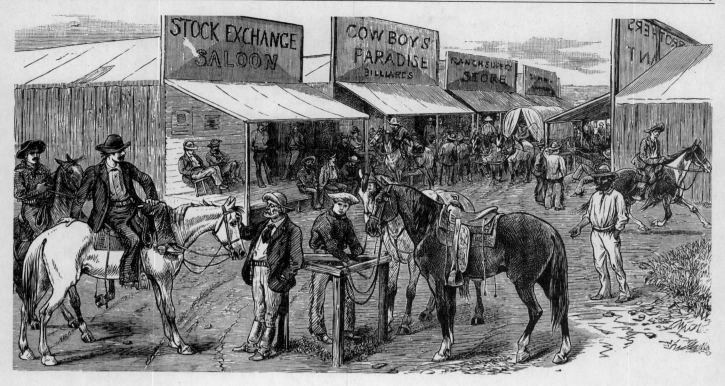

A Way of Life Ends

The railroads brought many good things to the white settlers of the Great Plains. But they brought little good to the Plains Indians. Many of the Indians were **nomads.** They followed roaming buffalo herds, hunting them from horseback.

To the Plains Indians, the buffalo was life itself. No part of the animal was allowed to go to waste. The Indians ate buffalo meat. They used the skins for clothing and for coverings for their tents. They made tools and weapons from the bones. The sinew—the tough tissue that holds the muscles in place—was used for thread and for bowstrings. Buffalo droppings became fuel for the Indians' fires.

What would happen if the buffalo should disappear? This was almost too terrible to consider. The buffalo had always lived on the Great Plains, and it seemed it always would.

The End of the Buffalo

The railroad companies, however, saw things in a different light. They thought of the buffalo as a cheap source of food for their workers. But they also saw the buffalo as a troublesome pest. The animals needed large areas on which to graze. Sometimes they tore up track as they moved from one place to another. So the railroads began hiring hunters. One of them, "Buffalo Bill" Cody, killed more than 4,000 buffalo in 18 months while working for the Kansas Pacific Railroad.

Even after the railroads were built, the killing continued. Shooting buffalo became a popular sport. Bored travelers on the railroads would lean out their windows and blast away at them.

In the 1860s, there had been almost 15 million buffalo on the Great Plains. In 1868 a Kansas Pacific train had to wait eight hours for a single herd to cross its tracks. Yet by the 1890s, there were no more than a few thousand of the animals left. Said one hunter, "A man could have walked 20 miles on their dead bodies."

The Native Americans lost still more than their main source of life. The settlers built fences, and this made travel across the Plains very difficult. The land itself was being taken from the Indians.

The United States wrote treaties which forced the Indians onto reservations. The government had set aside for them areas it thought no one else would want. The Indians had to sign papers which promised that they would be left alone "for as long as grass grows or water runs." However, most of the treaties were soon broken. One of the reasons for this was that gold and silver were discovered on reservation lands.

The Indians began to believe they had to fight to keep their way of life. Some, such as the Sioux and the Cheyenne, began attacking groups of miners and farmers.

The Indians had one great victory. In 1876, thousands of Sioux gathered in Montana along the Little Big Horn River. An American army force led by Colonel George Custer rode into the **ambush** and was wiped out.

The Sioux did not enjoy their victory for long. The army had too many soldiers and too many modern arms. In a few months, it defeated the Sioux and forced them back onto the reservations. Many white Americans felt ashamed at what had happened to the Plains Indians. Said one general, "We took away their country and their means of support. We broke up their way of living, their habit of life. It was for this that they made war. Could anyone expect less?"

George Custer

Chief Joseph

Chief Joseph, leader of the Nez Percé, had never wanted war. But in 1877, a few Nez Percé braves killed some whites. The army came after them. Was there any hope? For Chief Joseph there was only one answer: Canada. He led his people on a trip of more than 1,700 miles through the western mountains. Time after time, the soldiers caught up with them, only to be driven off. Just 40 miles from the Canadian border, Chief Joseph and his tired and starving band stopped to rest. Here the army caught up with them again. The Nez Percé held their ground for days, even though there were many more soldiers. However, Chief Joseph was finally forced to surrender. He said, "I am tired. . . . My heart is sick and sad. . . . I will fight no more forever."

The Last March of Chief Joseph

EXERCISE 9

Complete each statement below. Write the letter of the word or words that make it correct.

a. Ireland
b. nomads
c. Chief Joseph
d. transcontinental
e. George Custer
f. Great Plains
g. Omaha, Nebraska

h. Sacramento, California
i. Buffalo Bill Cody
j. Germany
k. golden spike
l. China
m. buffalo

1. The Union Pacific and Central Pacific railroads met in 1869 to form the first _____ railroad in the United States.

2. The Central Pacific had started laying track near _____ . The Union Pacific had started in _____ .

3. Many of the workers on the Central Pacific were immigrants from _____ . Most of the Union Pacific workers were American blacks and immigrants from _____ and _____ .

4. On May 10, 1869, a _____ was hammered in at Promontory Point in Utah.

5. The land between the Mississippi River and the Rocky Mountains is known as the _____ .

6. People who do not live in one place but move around as they hunt are called _____ .

7. Many of the Plains Indians depended for life on roving herds of _____ .

8. The American army force at Little Big Horn was led by _____ .

9. _____ was a famous hunter for the railroads.

10. _____ was the leader of the Nez Percé on their flight to escape the American army.

Answer the following questions.

11. What were some of the difficulties faced by those who built the first transcontinental railroad?

_____

_____

_____

_____

12. By the 1890s, what had happened to the land between the Mississippi and the Rockies?

_____

_____

13. Why was the buffalo so important to the Indians?

_____

_____

_____

_____

_____

_____

_____

14. How did the railroad companies look upon the buffalo?

_____

_____

_____

15. What is one of the reasons treaties between Indians and whites were broken?

_____

_____

Chapter 10

A New Age for Industry

He had already **invented** the **phonograph.** Now Thomas Edison wanted to light up America's cities. Some of the world's greatest minds had been trying for years to use **electricity** to produce light. Edison was sure he could do what no one else had ever done. He was sure he could make small lights for use in homes and offices.

Edison wanted to run a **current** through a thin thread set in a glass bulb. He spent two years searching for the right kind of thread or wire. He tried everything he could think of—gold, silver, cloth, wool, animal hair, human hair. No matter what he put in the bulb, it wouldn't stay lit. He sent people to Japan and to the jungles of the Amazon. Nothing they brought back worked.

Night after night, Edison and his helpers stayed up late, trying one thing after another. Everyone was ready to give up—everyone, that is, but Edison. One December night in 1879, he tried putting some burned cotton thread in the bulb. Since nothing else had worked, he didn't really expect that this would. But it did. When the current was turned on, the bulb lit up the workshop. And it stayed lit. It burned through the night and into the next day. It went out only when Edison put some extra current through the wire.

Something that looked almost like magic was about to affect people everywhere.

Edison did not want his invention to be only for the rich. He wanted as many people as possible to be able to light their homes. He built a power station in New York in 1882 that sent electricity to homes and businesses. "We'll make electric light so cheap," he said, "that only the rich will be able to burn candles."

By the early 1900s, many homes, offices, and stores had electric lights. No longer did families have to use candles at night. No longer did students have to read by oil lamps. Now they simply flicked a switch to get a bright, steady light.

Thomas Edison

New Ways for a Changing America

At one time, nearly everything had been made of wood or iron. Power came from human or animal muscle or from steam. In the new America, there were office buildings, railroads, bridges, and factories. They were made with steel. The energy that was needed to keep everything running was now coming from coal, oil, and electricity.

In the 1850s, inventors found cheaper ways to make large amounts of steel from iron and coal. This led to the birth of new industries. One industry was started to dig more iron ore and coal out of the ground. Another industry melted these two together to produce the steel.

Wherever there was a large group of factories, a city grew up around it. As we have already noted, the cities were magnets that attracted people seeking jobs. Older cities became larger. New cities sprang up where there had been only small towns. People needed food and clothing and homes. New businesses supplied these needs. America was becoming a land of big cities.

Exciting things were happening in the cities. Edison's electric light lit up the outdoors as well as the indoors. People could stay out later at night. Theaters, restaurants, circuses, and concerts made urban life interesting and different.

Alexander Graham Bell

All over America, new inventions were changing people's lives. Alexander Graham Bell had wondered if electricity could carry the human voice over a wire. In 1876, after years of work, he had come up with something he called the telephone. Service began at New Haven, Connecticut, in 1878 with 21 **customers.** Thirty years later, millions had phones.

The manufacture of steel beams meant that the cities could grow upwards. The first **skyscraper** was built in Chicago in the 1880s. It reached the amazing height of ten stories. With the invention of electric elevators, the buildings soon went even higher.

The cities stretched out as well as up. Electric streetcars and railroads were built. They made it possible for people to live farther away from their jobs.

"Don't Be Afraid to Work"

John D. Rockefeller

For many years, people in western Pennsylvania had noticed an oily liquid that dripped from between the rocks. The Indians and some pioneers had used it for medicine.

In the 1860s, people started using this oil for heating and lighting. This was the start of another new industry. Thousands of people rushed to the oil fields. They were all trying to strike it rich.

One of those who went to the oil fields was a young man named John D. Rockefeller. He saw, as few others did, just how important oil would become. Working out of Cleveland, Ohio, he started his own **refinery.** Things went well, and Rockefeller started buying other refineries. By the age of 35, he owned most of the refineries in the country. He also owned drilling fields, pipelines, and tank cars. His company, Standard Oil, was one of the largest in the United States. And John D. Rockefeller became one of the wealthiest men in the world.

Rockefeller often said, "Don't be afraid to work." He took his own advice seriously, working days, months, and years without a break. However, not everyone was able to profit by this advice as well as Rockefeller did. Most people worked long and hard at their jobs for very little money.

Many people worked 6 days a week for 12 or 13 hours a day. The factories were dark, dirty, and dangerous. Children also worked, sometimes for as little as 25 cents a day. Those that did had little time to study or play.

Later, laws were made to protect children. But the factories remained terrible places. There was no such thing as a **vacation.** Workers who were hurt on the job were not paid. Workers who got sick were not paid. Anyone who asked for higher pay or who demanded better conditions might be fired.

One worker alone had little power to change things for the better. But many acting together might be able to bring about changes. Labor unions were formed for this purpose. These were groups of workers who fought together for better conditions and higher pay.

The unions did help many workers. But the struggles were hard. And the unions did not always win. In fact, in the beginning, they often lost.

Factory work

Violence at Homestead

The Homestead Steel Works in Pennsylvania was one of the toughest places a person could work. In the furnace room, large burners threw out fire and sparks. Men worked within inches of melted steel and often were badly burned. Those who were injured were taken off the payroll.

In 1892, the Homestead **employees** were told that the company was going to cut their **wages.** They decided to go out on strike.

The owners of the mill were not going to give in. A 12-foot high fence was put up around the mill. New workers were hired. Guards were brought in to keep the mill in operation. When the guards tried to enter the mill, a bloody fight broke out. Nine strikers and seven guards were killed. The state government did not support the workers. It sent troops to Homestead to keep the mill open and arrest strikers. The company took back some workers but refused to take back many of the strikers. Those who could not get their jobs back had to seek work in another town in the middle of winter. Those who could return to their jobs found that their pay had been cut almost in half.

The union movement suffered from this defeat. Factory owners all over America held out against the unions. It would be years before the government and the owners were willing to accept them. Only then were workers able to win decent wages and working conditions.

EXERCISE 10

Study the chart below. Then answer the questions that follow.

1870	The Standard Oil Company was founded.
1873	The typewriter was invented.
1876	Alexander Graham Bell invented the telephone.
1877	Thomas Edison invented the phonograph.
1879	Thomas Edison invented the electric light bulb.
1882	The streets of New York City were lit by electricity.
1883	The first skyscraper was built in Chicago.
1886	The American Federation of Labor (a national labor union) was founded.
1892	The Homestead Strike broke out.
1895	The radio was invented.

1. How many years does the time line cover?

_____

2. How many inventions are listed on the time line?

_____

3. Which of these inventions were made by Thomas Edison?

_____

4. Which of these events would you say was the most important? Why?

_____

_____

_____

5. Which event on this time line was made possible by the invention of the electric lightbulb?

_____

_____

6. In which event on this time line did John D. Rockefeller play a very large role?

_____

Decide whether the following statements are true or false. Write T beside those that are true and F beside those that are false.

7. _____ Thomas Edison's light bulb stayed lit when he passed an electric current through a strand of hair.

8. _____ Edison said his invention was mainly for the rich.

9. _____ Before there were light bulbs, people lit their homes with candles and oil lamps.

10. _____ It wasn't until the middle of the 20th century that electricity was used in homes and businesses.

11. _____ Steel is made from iron and gold.

12. _____ People who lived in the cities started going to bed earlier when their streets were lit with electricity.

13. _____ Those who use or buy goods or services are known as customers.

14. _____ Electric streetcars made it possible for workers to live farther from their jobs.

15. _____ In the 1920s, there were very few telephones.

16. _____ Before oil was used for heating and lighting, it was used as a medicine.

17. _____ Unions were formed to bring about better working conditions.

18. _____ Workers often won their early union struggles.

19. _____ An employee is a person who works for someone else.

Chapter 11

A Nation of Immigrants

For two stormy weeks, the *Polynesia* had been steaming across the Atlantic. On the morning of May 18, 1893, Mary Antin had her first view of America.

First she saw trees. As the ship got closer, she saw the tops of buildings. The ship steamed slowly into the New York harbor. In Russia, the old country, Mary Antin had never seen a building taller than four stories. But before her now were buildings that stretched 25 stories into the sky. There were boats everywhere in the busy harbor. Off to the left, on Liberty Island, was the Statue of Liberty. It was now eight years since the statue had been built. To Mary it seemed a perfect symbol of the powerful and free new country she was entering.

Everyone crowded to the rail to get a better look. It was a sight they would never forget.

In 1912, in her book *The Promised Land*, Mary Antin referred to that moment. She wrote, ". . . at last I was going to America! Really, really going, at last! . . . The winds rushed in from outer space, roaring in my ears, America! America!"

The ship docked, and Mary saw her father. He had left Russia three years earlier and had settled in Boston. There he had saved enough money to send for Mary, her mother, two sisters, and a brother. He threw his arms around his family and smiled happily. "So now you are all Americans," he said.

The Golden Door

Like many millions of others, Mary Antin was an immigrant to the United States. This is a "nation of immigrants," of people born in other places. In the last 200 years, more people have come to this country to live than to any other. Most (more than 35 million) entered the United States during the 80 years between 1840 and 1920.

Before 1885, the immigrants came mainly from northern and western Europe. These people are known as the "Old Immigrants." They were from such places as Germany, England, and **Scandinavia.** They often settled in the central and western parts of the United States. Many Irish also arrived then. Most settled in Boston and New York and in the other eastern cities. Africans, as we have learned, were forced into slavery in the South.

During the 1880s, the numbers of immigrants greatly increased. Many came from the countries of southern and eastern Europe—from Greece, Italy, Hungary, Austria, Poland, and Russia. By the 1890s, millions of "New Immigrants" (those who came after 1885) were flowing into the United States each year.

Like the Old Immigrants, the New Immigrants came to the United States for several different reasons. They came to escape poverty and hunger and because they were ruled by unjust governments. While the Old Immigrants worked mostly at farming, many of the New Immigrants worked in the factories and mines of a growing America.

European immigrant

Whether they sailed across the Atlantic or the Pacific, the New Immigrants came by steamship. Because they were generally poor, most spent the ocean trip in steerage, the cheapest and most uncomfortable part of the ship. Steerage passengers stayed close to the waterline in dark and dirty quarters. Their **voyage** was difficult. Many got sick; some died. But these people were bound for America, willing to risk everything. They were taking their hopes with them.

The Strange and the New

It would be a while, however, before their dreams could become real. The new land seemed very strange to the immigrants. In the cities, everything moved quickly. People spoke and dressed in ways the newcomers hadn't known before. Even the churches, schools, and stores were different from those in the old country.

Usually, the immigrants moved into parts of the cities where they could live among other people from their homelands. Neighborhoods called Little Italy, Little Poland, and Little China (later to be known as Chinatown) sprang up. Here customs, **diets,** and **languages** were kept alive.

Most of the immigrants were poor. Many did not speak a word of English. Often they had come from farming villages and were not used to living in crowded apartments.

New York City, 1897

As more and more immigrants entered the cities, there were not enough places for them to live. Old buildings soon became too crowded. New buildings called tenements were put up quickly and cheaply. They were often dark and narrow and had poor lighting. Landlords crowded families into small rooms. In one block of New York City in the 1890s, 577 people lived in just 97 rooms.

If things were so bad, why did people continue to come here? America was the land of **opportunity.** The immigrants had lost the hope of bettering themselves in the countries they'd left. This was the place where they and their children would have a new start in life.

Sometimes the immigrants faced so much **prejudice** that it was hard to stay hopeful. Many people from Asia had settled along the Pacific coast—in Washington, Oregon, and California. As we read in Chapter 9, many of the Chinese found work building the railroads. Others worked in the gold fields of the West. But soon there were no jobs on the railroads or in the gold fields. Some Asians returned to their original homes. Others took jobs in the West Coast cities and towns. Because they needed the money so badly, many Asians were willing to work for lower wages. This made many white Americans angry.

Other immigrants faced many of the same problems. For years, the United States had welcomed them. But as time went on, a lot of Americans changed their minds. They started to believe the immigrants—whose salaries were kept low—would get the jobs that they thought they should have. Others did not like the new citizens because they found their customs and habits, their ways of life strange. People seemed to have forgotten that the United States was built up by immigrants or "outsiders." And unless we are Native Americans, we are all outsiders.

In the 1880s, anti-immigrant groups were formed. On the West Coast, many Chinese who owned stores or land were beaten or even killed. In 1882, a federal law stopped Chinese workers from coming into the country. During the 1920s only about 350,000 immigrants a year were allowed in. In 1929, the number was cut to 150,000. People from northern and western Europe were permitted to enter before people from other parts of the world. Most Africans and Asians were kept out entirely. The great golden doors that had welcomed people from all over the world were being pulled shut.

The Golden Door Closes

Immigrants still come to the United States, though not in the same huge numbers they once did. In recent years, many people from Mexico, Southeast Asia, and Central America have come to live here. Like the immigrants of 100 years ago, they have brought new ways to these shores. They have made our life richer. America's mix of cultures, talents, and skills is one of our greatest sources of strength.

The Strength of Our Differences

EXERCISE 11

Complete each statement below. Write the letter of the word or words that make it correct.

a. Statue of Liberty

b. northern and western

c. new start in life

d. *The Promised Land*

e. steerage

f. southern and eastern

g. cities

h. Mexico, Southeast Asia, and Central America

1. One of the sights Mary Antin would always remember seeing when she entered the United States was the _____ . Years later she wrote about her journey in a book called _____ .

2. At first, most of the people who came to the United States came from _____ Europe.

3. During the 1880s, most of the people came from _____ Europe.

4. During the early immigration, many Irish settled in the _____ in the East.

5. The cheapest and most uncomfortable part of a steamship is known as _____ .

6. People came to the United States because they wanted a _____ .

7. In recent years, many immigrants have come to the United States from _____ .

Answer the questions below.

8. What kind of work did most of the Old Immigrants do?

_____

9. What kind of work did many of the New Immigrants do?

_____

10. What are three things that both the Old and the New Immigrants wished to leave behind?

_____

_____

_____

11. What are some of the difficulties that were faced by the newcomers to America?

_____

_____

_____

_____

_____

_____

12. Why did Americans change their minds about the people who were coming here?

_____

_____

_____

_____

_____

13. By the 1920s, which groups of people were kept out of the country almost entirely?

_____

Chapter 12

The Age of Reform

Words to Know

accident something that wasn't expected to happen

bribe money given to get someone to do something against the law

consumer one who buys goods or services

illegal against the law

investigation a search for facts

jingle a catchy tune

rival one who tries to do something better than someone else

Mary had a little lamb,
And when she saw it sicken,
She shipped it off to Packingtown,
And now it's labeled chicken.

Packingtown was the name given to the stockyards of Chicago. Cattle from throughout the West were taken there to be killed. The meat was either packed, turned into sausage, or smoked. Then it was sent to hungry cities all over the country.

The writer Upton Sinclair had heard the **jingle** about Packingtown. But he didn't think it was very funny. He had an idea that some very strange things were going on there. He decided to go into the stockyards to report on them to the public.

Sinclair saw sick animals being slaughtered with healthy ones. He found meat scraps lying on dirty floors. The floors were damp and soggy, and workers spat on them when they felt the need. Rotting meat was scooped up with the remains of poisoned rats and with pieces of rope and wood. This was made into sausage and canned ham. Sinclair also found that government health inspectors were taking **bribes** to ignore the filthy conditions.

When Sinclair finished his **investigation,** he felt he would never again eat meat. He decided to write a book that would tell people just what they were putting into themselves. Even more than this, he wanted people to know about working conditions in the plants. In his novel *The Jungle*, published in

1906, Sinclair wrote, "It was a nasty job killing these sick cows, for when you plunged your knife into them they would burst and splash foul-smelling stuff into your face. . . . It was enough to make anybody sick, to think people had to eat such stuff as this. But they must be eating it—for the canners were going on preparing it, year after year."

Sinclair's writings shocked the country into action. President Theodore Roosevelt and the Congress passed the Pure Food and Drug Act. Said Sinclair, "I aimed at the public's heart and by **accident** I hit it in the stomach." *The Jungle* didn't improve the lot of the stockyard workers. But it made a difference in the quality of the food Americans ate.

The Reformers

The early 1900s were an exciting time in America. There was a strong feeling that honest citizens could make positive changes in society. People like Upton Sinclair were writing and speaking about the problems they saw around them. Those who worked for change, who wanted to make America a better place, were known as reformers. Today we call the period in which they lived the Age of Reform.

As industry expanded, some people had become very wealthy. The mansions of the rich could be seen in any city. Yet close by were the most terrible slums, where people lived in poverty and sickness.

Most Americans believed that business people should be free to make whatever deals they wanted. Now, however, things had gotten out of hand. Some companies had become giants. With their wealth and size, they could buy out many of the smaller companies. A few large companies ran whole industries. They had formed groups called trusts, which controlled practically everything that went on. They'd raise the prices **consumers** paid for goods and lower the salaries of the workers who produced the goods.

The country had never been against the idea of anyone's making a lot of money by working hard. But the trusts seemed to be going too far. That's how Ida Tarbell felt, and she decided to do something about it.

Upton Sinclair

Ida Tarbell

Ida Tarbell was one of the leading writers of her day. Since she wrote histories, her main interest was in the past. But she also had reason to be interested in the present. Her father had once run a small oil company. Then he had been forced out of business by Standard Oil. Ida Tarbell spent five years investigating John D. Rockefeller's company. In 1902, she began writing about it.

Standard was the largest oil refining company in the world. Ida Tarbell's study, *History of the Standard Oil Company* (1904), showed how it got that way. She discovered, for instance, that there were secret deals between the oil company and the railroads. Standard had forced the railroads to give back some of the money that had been paid to them to have the oil shipped. The rail companies then had to charge the other oil companies more for this service. Rockefeller was able to sell his oil at a cheaper rate. His **rivals** lost their customers and were forced to sell their businesses to Standard Oil. The owner of one refinery said, "There was only one buyer on the market, and we had to sell at their terms."

To most Americans, what had happened was wrong. When they read Ida Tarbell's reports, they began demanding controls on unfair business practices. This resulted in anti-trust laws, which made these kinds of practices **illegal**.

Jacob Riis

As a police reporter for a New York City newspaper, Jacob Riis saw life at its hardest. In 1890, his book *How the Other Half Lives* described some of the problems the cities were facing. In it he wrote about an ordinary slum building. "Be careful! The hall is dark and you might fall over the children pitching pennies there. Not that it would hurt them. They get kicks and slaps every day. They don't have much else. That woman you just bumped into was filling her buckets from the outside hydrants. The people who live here have their sinks in the halls, not their apartments. Everyone on the floor uses one sink. In summer, the terrible smells from the sinks poison everyone."

While Jacob Riis showed Americans how grim the poorer parts of their cities had become, Jane Addams helped poor city dwellers learn the skills needed to improve their lives.

Jane Addams grew up in a wealthy part of Chicago. As a young girl, she was given almost anything she wanted. She had no idea how bad things were just a few miles from her home. But then she saw her first slum. Other rich young people had seen the slums and had chosen to turn their backs on them. But Jane Addams promised herself that she would do what she could to help those who lived there.

At the age of 29, she shocked her family by moving into one of Chicago's slums. "Why must you live there?" her mother asked her. Addams answered simply, "There are people there who need help, and I want to help them."

Jane Addams founded a settlement house called Hull House. Here there were nursery schools, gyms, and a playground. There were college-level courses and classes in reading and writing and in crafts like bookmaking. There were doctors and nurses. There were theater programs, music groups, and social clubs. Hull House even had a summer camp in the country. People came from around the world to study how Hull House was helping the people of Chicago.

When people praised Jane Addams, she'd look at them in a funny way. She'd say, "Think what I have gained! Think how I have grown!" If joy and understanding were the gifts she gave, they were also the gifts she received.

These were the reformers, who were also known as the "progressives." The progress they worked for was meant to enrich the lives of all. They were fired with hope and trust in the future. It was in this spirit that the 20th century—the "American Century"—began.

Jane Addams

EXERCISE 12

Match each statement on the left with the person on the right who might have written or said it.

1. _____ "The Standard Oil
   Company uses unfair ways of
   getting control of the oil
   industry."

2. _____ "It was a nasty job
   killing these sick cows, for
   when you plunged your knife
   into them they would burst
   and splash foul-smelling stuff
   into your face."

3. _____ "Be careful! The hall is
   dark and you might fall over
   the children pitching pennies
   there. Not that it would hurt
   them. They get kicks and slaps
   every day."

4. _____ "Mary had a little lamb,
   And when she saw it sicken,
   She shipped it off to Packingtown,
   And now it's labeled chicken."

5. _____ "Think what I have
   gained! Think how I have
   grown!"

a. Jacob Riis

b. people of
   Chicago making
   fun of the
   stockyards

c. Upton Sinclair

d. Jane Addams

e. Ida Tarbell

6. Go to the library and read further about one of the reformers mentioned in this chapter. Write a short report on his or her life. Include your thoughts on whatever *you* find most interesting about that person. Begin your report here.

_____

_____

_____

_____

_____

_____

_____

_____

_____

_____

_____

_____

_____

_____

_____

_____

_____

_____

_____

_____

_____

_____

_____